Branch Lines
in
Kent

Peter A. Hardir

GW00577989

R1 class 0-6-0T No.31147 pulling a goods train through Clowes Wood on the Whitstable & Canterbury Railway. May 17th 1952.　　　J.J.Smith

Published by Peter A. Harding,
Mossgiel, Bagshot Road, Knaphill,
Woking, Surrey GU21 2SG.

ISBN 0 9523458 1 1

© Peter A. Harding 1996.
Printed by Binfield Printers Ltd.,
Binfield Road, Byfleet, Surrey KT14 7PN.

Contents

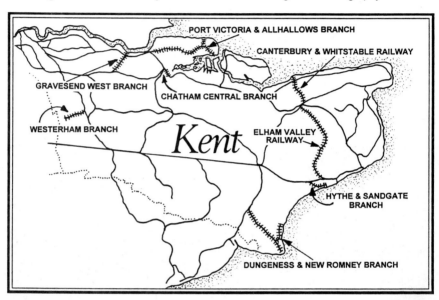

Brasted Station on the Westerham branch. September 15th 1957.   A.E.Bennett

Introduction

In a previous publication *The Col. Stephens Railways in Kent*, I covered the lines which Holman F. Stephens was involved with in that county, namely the Cranbrook & Paddock Wood Railway (later known as the Hawkhurst branch line), the Rother Valley Railway (later known as the Kent & East Sussex Railway), the Sheppey Light Railway, and finally the East Kent Light Railway.

As a companion to that publication, I would now like to take a similar look at the other branch lines in Kent.

Most of the lines were built out of a long standing feud between the two major companies in the county, the South Eastern Railway (SER), under the chairmanship of Sir Edward Watkin, and his opposite number at the London, Chatham & Dover Railway (LCDR), James Staats Forbes. These two gentlemen became bitter rivals towards the latter part of the nineteenth century, and were responsible for the building of several railways purely as a defensive measure to stop entry into each others territory. Although the LCDR only built one of the lines which we will cover (the Gravesend West branch), they certainly knew how to manipulate the SER into action by implying that they were interested in building a line in a certain area. For their part, the SER would often encourage a local company to put up the money and, when all was up and running (normally using SER locomotives), they would soon absorb the local company into their own system.

Although built under these circumstances, there was nearly always an ulterior motive behind each project. i.e. ports at Dungeness and Port Victoria; an easier route to Folkestone Harbour via Hythe and Sandgate; a link up with the London, Tilbury & Southend Railway via a tunnel under the Thames from the Gravesend West branch; a quicker route from Canterbury to Folkestone etc.

Nevertheless, there is no doubt that all these lines had their own charm and character but, with just two minor exceptions, very little evidence remains of their former glory and are now all but a fading memory. I hope that this publication brings back to mind the time when the branch line trains puffed and blew their way through fields and woods in the Kentish countryside.

C class 0-6-0 No.31682 at Southfleet Station with a goods train on the Gravesend West branch. November 21st 1959. J.J.Smith

Historical Background

The long running feud between Sir Edward Watkin of the SER and his counterpart James Staats Forbes at the LCDR, resulted in the construction of several branch lines in Kent which under normal circumstances should never have been built. The Chatham Central branch is one such line that readily springs to mind. The legendary disputes between Watkin and Forbes were not only confined to the villages and small towns in Kent but were also to take place in the tunnels below London, as Watkin was also chairman of the Metropolitan Railway, while Forbes was also chairman of the Metropolitan District Railway.

In the early days, the SER were poised to take over their smaller rival the East Kent Railway (the original title of the LCDR), but missed their chance and allowed the East Kent Railway to grow in stature, extending their main line to Dover and changing their name to the London, Chatham & Dover Railway. During the next few years the SER and the LCDR almost agreed a working arrangement on several occasions, but once Watkin and Forbes became the respective chairmen, the feud took hold, and it was not until Watkin retired in 1894 that the rivalry ended. In 1898 both companies agreed to work together but remain separate under the heading of the South Eastern & Chatham Railway Management Committee (SE&CR). From this time onwards, Forbes became a 'technical advisor' to the SE&CR until he died in 1904.

Once the SE&CR became a working partnership, they looked at some of the lines which had resulted from the feud, and decided that the Chatham Central branch was one line which was now no longer required and closed it on and from October 1st 1911. All other lines described in this publication continued under the SE&CR who, after the 1923 grouping, became part of the newly formed Southern Railway.

Several changes took place under the Southern Railway, including the construction of the Allhallows branch from a junction on the Port Victoria line, closure of the Elham Valley line, closure to passengers on the Canterbury & Whitstable Railway, closure of the section of line between Hythe and Sandgate, plus re-siting a section of the New Romney branch.

In 1948, the Southern Railway became British Railways Southern Region after nationalisation and, over the next few years, the new owners soon closed the remaining branches, apart from the section of the New Romney branch towards Dungeness Power Station and the line towards Port Victoria which remains open for carrying oil, ballast and cement.

Sir Edward Watkin (1819-1901)

Sir Edward Watkin was born near Manchester on September 26th 1819, the son of a Manchester cotton merchant. In his youth, he joined the family business and developed an interest in politics. His railway career began in 1845 when he left the family business and joined the Trent Valley Railway as secretary. This company was absorbed by the London & North Western Railway in 1846 and Watkin became head of its branch lines department, and then assistant to the general manager, Captain Mark Huish. In 1854 he left the London & North Western Railway to join a rival company - the Manchester, Sheffield & Lincolnshire Railway as general manager and, by 1861, he was also connected with nine smaller railway companies in some form of capacity.

Later in 1861, Watkin left the Manchester, Sheffield & Lincolnshire Railway to go to Canada and advise the Grand Trunk Railway Company, of which he soon became their president.

Although his work with the Grand Trunk Railway was not a great success, he was at the head of a British syndicate which bought the Hudson Bay Company and refloated it for a large profit.

After returning to England, Watkin was elected to the board of the Great Western Railway, and his former company the Manchester, Sheffield & Lincolnshire Railway, becoming their chairman in 1864. In 1865, he joined the SER and was elected chairman in 1866. For his previous services in Canada, he was knighted in 1868. In 1872 he joined the board of the Metropolitan Railway and became their chairman.

From 1880, Watkin spent much of his time on two projects which were very close to his heart. First, a rail link from Manchester to Paris via a channel tunnel. Second, a 'Watkin' Tower to be built at Wembley Park, Middlesex, to rival the Eiffel Tower in Paris. Both schemes failed, but as we shall see later, the idea of a port at Dungeness was considered by Watkin as a possible alternative to the channel tunnel, while only the first stage of the tower project was completed and opened to the public in 1896, but due to the lack of funds, this was as far as the tower went and the completed stage was demolished in 1907.

Watkin, who was Liberal MP for Stockport from 1864 to 1868 and for Hythe in Kent from 1874 to 1895, died at Rose Hill, Northenden, Cheshire, on April 13th 1901 aged eighty-two.

Sir Edward Watkin.   James Staats Forbes.

James Staats Forbes (1823-1904)

James Staats Forbes was born in Aberdeen on March 7th 1823. He was educated at Woolwich and trained as an engineer, beginning his working life in the office of Isambard Kingdom Brunel. At the age of eighteen, he joined the Great Western Railway as a booking clerk at Paddington, moving to Gloucester as district goods superintendent in 1855. On leaving the Great Western Railway, he took on the responsibility of a five year contract as managing director of the Dutch Rhenish Railway Co., which was owned and managed by British capitalists.

Forbes joined the LCDR as general manager in April 1861 and after the company had run into financial difficulties in 1866, he spearheaded a successful rescue operation. In 1871 he joined the LCDR board and in 1873 became chairman. Forbes was also appointed part-time managing director of the Metropolitan District Railway in 1870, becoming chairman from 1872 to 1901.

At the same time he was involved with several other railway companies, including the Didcot, Newbury & Southampton Railway, as well as foreign hotels, mortgage companies and other overseas railways. He helped to promote many other companies, including the Anglo French Fire Insurance Company, the Swan Electric Light Co., the London Electricity Supply Corporation, and the very successful National Telephone Co.

James Staats Forbes, who unsuccessfully stood for Parliament, as a Liberal candidate for Dover in 1874, died on April 5th 1904 aged eighty-one.

The Canterbury & Whitstable Railway

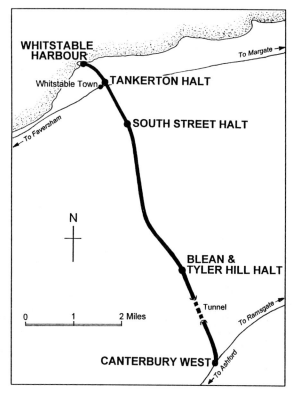

Although a typical Kentish branch line in appearance, the real claim to fame of the Canterbury & Whitstable Railway is that it was the first public steam powered passenger and goods railway in the South of England and was opened in 1830, the same year as the Liverpool & Manchester Railway.

In 1823, William James, one of the pioneers of railways at the time, visited Canterbury and suggested to the City Council, that as they were experiencing transport problems, they should think of a railway link from Canterbury to the Thames estuary. James surveyed several routes from Canterbury to Whitstable and finally settled on one.

A new company was soon set up and on June 10th 1825, an Act incorporating the Canterbury & Whitstable Railway received the Royal Assent.

As there was some confusion over the estimate for building the line that James had suggested, George Stephenson was called in to become the line's engineer, although he delegated the laying of the track to Joseph Locke (who later became engineer to the London & Southampton Railway), and appointed John Dixon of Darlington as resident engineer.

Through lack of funds, work on the railway came to a stand still in 1827, after the Tyler Hill Tunnel had been constructed and, at this time, John Dixon left the company. When new financial arrangements were made, Robert Stephenson took charge and appointed Joshua Richardson to replace John Dixon as resident engineer. The line was soon completed and the ceremonial opening was on May 3rd 1830, with public traffic starting the following day.

The line was very steeply graded and was to depend on two stationary steam engines to haul trains by cable. One was at the top of Tyler Hill and the other one was at Clowes Wood.

The famous locomotive "Invicta", which was built by Robert Stephenson, was brought by sea to Whitstable in 1830 and was intended to be used only over the last $1^3/4$ miles at the Whitstable end of the line. In 1839, "Invicta" was replaced by four strong horses after proving unsuitable, while the rest of the line was worked by cable, with a third stationary engine installed at Bogshole.

Because of financial problems in 1838, the Canterbury & Whitstable Railway Company leased the line to a company called Nicholson & Bayless but, in 1841 Nicholson & Bayless became bankrupt, and from then on, the Canterbury & Whitstable Railway Company tried to let the line once again. They could not find an interested party until 1844, when the SER took over the running of the line, and it eventually became part of their system.

Once the SER took control, they soon decided that the whole line should be relaid with heavier track, and in 1846, conventional steam locomotives took over entirely. Modifications took place at both ends of the line, when a new harbour station opened at Whitstable, and it was also decided to divert passenger trains at the other end of the line into the SER's station (known later as Canterbury West) on their new Ashford to Ramsgate line, retaining the original terminus for goods traffic.

In 1894, Whitstable Harbour Station closed and a new station was opened on the opposite side of Harbour Street. By 1898 the SER had linked with the LCDR and had formed the SE&CR.

An unidentified R class 0-6-0T approaching Canterbury from Whitstable with a mixed train.

Lens of Sutton

7

One of the main features of the line was Tyler Hill Tunnel, which had a very limited bore. This meant that after conventional locomotives were introduced in 1846, only Tayleur 119 class 0-6-0's could be used. In 1883, two Stirling O class 0-6-0's with cut-down chimneys worked the line until 1890, when four Stirling R class 0-6-0 tank engines, built by the SER at Ashford and given cut-down chimneys, worked the line until it closed.

In 1908, a small wooden halt was opened at Tyler Hill and on June 1st 1911, a similar halt was opened at South Street, just over a mile south of Whitstable. A third halt was opened at Tankerton in July 1914.

In 1923 the SE&CR became part of the newly formed Southern Railway at the grouping and, although things carried on very much as before, the competition from road transport became very noticeable and it was decided to withdraw the passenger service on and from January 2nd 1931. The goods traffic was still in a healthy situation and continued with as many as four trains each day.

The line passed into the hands of the newly formed British Railways Southern Region after nationalisation in 1948, and because of the neglected state of the harbour at Whitstable, the daily goods train from Canterbury was no longer required. The line soon became neglected, with weeds growing between the tracks.

After much speculation, "is one of our original railways about to close ?", British Railways finally decided to close the line completely, and a final train consisting of R class 0-6-0 No. 31010 and two brake vans ran on December 1st 1952.

This was in fact not the end, because in February 1953, after the floods which hit the East Coast of Britain had caused damage to the main Kent Coast railway line, the Whitstable & Canterbury Railway was reopened to carry essential goods while the main line was repaired. This temporary service began on February 5th and lasted for twenty three days before the line finally closed.

South Street Halt, looking towards Whitstable.   Lens of Sutton

R1 class 0-6-0T No.31069 crosses the north Kent main line with the branch goods train, while King Arthur class 4-6-0 *Sir Dodinas Le Savage* heads the Victoria-Ramsgate express.

The late Dr.P.Ransome-Wallis

R1 class 0-6-0T No.31010 emerging from the southern portal of Tyler Hill tunnel.

The late Dr.P.Ransome-Wallis

The Hythe & Sandgate Branch

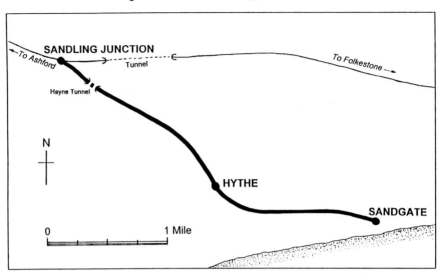

When the SER built their main line from Ashford to Folkestone, they settled on a more inland route, missing out Hythe, which was considered at the time more important than Folkestone. Hythe was not only a resort and market town, but also one of the Cinque Ports containing several military camps nearby.

Later, as sea front developments at Seabrook and Sandgate started to link Hythe and Folkestone, the SER decided in 1864 to promote a branch from the main line, at a junction near Westerhanger, to run through Hythe to Sandgate, although it was not until January 27th 1870, that the SER helped to form the Hythe & Sandgate Railway Company, who would own the land, while the SER would provide the finance for the new railway.

The engineer was the SER's Francis Brady and the appointed contractor was Philip Stiff of Dover, although he never actually finished the work and the SER paid him off and completed the job with their own workforce.

The line was 3¹/₂ miles long, double track and was formally opened on October 9th 1874 with trains starting from Westerhanger Station. In 1876, the SER obtained permission to extend the line from Sandgate, along the seashore to Folkestone Harbour which would be more direct and avoid the rather steep branch which already existed from Folkestone to the harbour. Unfortunately, this extension was never built but, if it had, this line would no doubt still be in use to this day.

In 1888, Sandling Junction Station was opened at the site of the junction. This new station had four platforms, two on the main Ashford - Folkestone line, and two on the branch. From Sandling Junction, the line ran past Saltwood Castle to Hythe Station, which was 1¹/₂ miles from the junction. From Hythe, the line continued under the cliffs until it reached Sandgate Station which was 3¹/₂ miles from the junction.

Apart from building the Sandgate branch, the SER later absorbed the Sandgate & Hythe Tramway, which was a standard gauge horse drawn tramway running for nearly four miles from the foot of Sandgate Hill along the coast to Hythe. It was completed and opened by the Folkestone, Sandgate & Hythe Tramway Co. in 1891 and was later nearly sold to the National Electric Construction Co. Ltd. to form part of a proposed Folkestone Tramway scheme which never materialised.

Although closed during the 1914-18 war, the Tramway reopened in 1919, but finally closed in 1921.

Locomotives used on the Sandgate branch when it first opened were Cudworth 118 class 2-4-0T's and Standard Goods 0-6-0's, followed by Stirling Q and Q1 class 0-4-4T's. In 1907, like many other similar branch lines in Kent, Wainwright Steam Railcars were introduced, but, as with other lines, they were not a success.

By 1916 the normal service was back in the hands of the Stirling Q and Q1's, and also his O and O1 class 0-6-0's, followed by Kirtley R and R1 class 0-4-4T's. From the 1930's, the push and pull units were regularly worked by former LB&SCR Stroudley D1 class 0-4-2T's and Billinton D3 class 0-4-4T's. The final years were in the hands of Wainwright H class 0-4-4T's. The goods traffic at this time was worked by either Stirling O1 class 0-6-0's or Wainwright C class 0-6-0's.

The section of the branch between Hythe and Sandgate was closed on and from April 1st 1931, and the whole branch was closed in 1943. It then reopened from Sandling Junction to Hythe in 1945. Final closure came on and from December 3rd 1951.

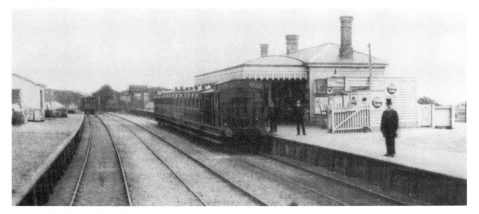

The station master stands proudly on the platform at Sandgate Station in 1891.   Lens of Sutton

Hythe Station.   Lens of Sutton

The short Hayne tunnel, looking south towards Hythe in 1937.   R.F.Roberts

D3 class 0-4-4T No.2365 with a push and pull set at Hythe Station in July 1938.   R.F.Roberts

The Westerham Branch

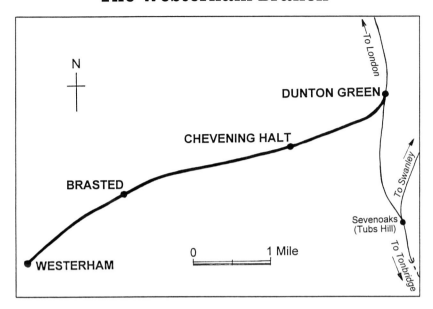

The inhabitants of the small market town of Westerham, which is situated in the wooded hills near the Surrey border, were hoping they would be connected to the railway as far back as 1864, when the SER had obtained permission to build a branch from their main line station at Dunton Green.

Although permission was renewed in 1867 and 1870, nothing happened and the local people became very impatient. So much so, that they promoted a Bill of their own in 1876, known as the Westerham Valley Railway (WVR). The proposed route for this railway was very similar to the SER's original Bill of 1864, with a line running from Dunton Green to Westerham via Brasted, but, unlike the SER line which would terminate at Westerham, the WVR proposal was to continue on and link up with the Croydon & Oxted line at Oxted.

As the WVR required the SER to work and maintain their line, the SER insisted that they would have nothing to do with the WVR unless they dropped the idea of the Westerham to Oxted section. After this was agreed, the WVR Bill went through Parliament on March 22nd 1876 and the SER chairman, Sir Edward Watkin became a director of the new WVR company, which was incorporated on July 24th 1876.

Work on the construction of the line began in October 1879 and the engineer appointed by the WVR was John William Grover while the contractor was Charles Chamber of Victoria Street, Westminster, London.

After a short delay during the latter part of 1880, due to heavy rain, the line was finally completed and ready for opening. Grand celebrations took place on Wednesday July 6th 1881, with a special train to Westerham conveying the directors of the WVR, followed by the time honoured English tradition of a luncheon. A special service of free trains continued for the rest of the day.

On the following day, Thursday July 7th 1881, the regular service commenced and this date is generally regarded as the official opening date. By August of the same year, the WVR ceased to exist and was absorbed by the SER.

The motive power which worked the branch in the early days was Cudworth 118 class 2-4-0's, but by the late 1890's, Stirling Q class 0-4-4T's had taken over the duties and occasionally the Stirling O class 0-6-0's could also be seen.

By 1906, the passenger service was handled by Wainwright Steam Railcars which the newly formed South Eastern & Chatham Railway had introduced as a form of economy on many of their branch lines. No's 3 and 7 were known to have worked the Westerham branch. As with the other branch lines, the introduction of Steam Railcars often meant the opening at remote locations, of simple wooden halts, which sometimes consisted of a small shelter. The Westerham branch gained one such halt between the villages of Chipstead and Chevening, which was opened on April 16th 1906 as Chevening Halt.

The Steam Railcars were not considered a great success on the Westerham branch, and were soon replaced by the returning Q class 0-4-4T's.

In 1909, the Wainwright P class 0-6-0T's were working the branch push and pull service, to be followed in the 1920's by Stirling B and B1 class 4-4-0's, and also Stirling O1 class 0-6-0's.

During the 1930's, Kirtley R and R1 class 0-4-4T's, took over branch line duties, working push and pull trains.

In 1936, the Sentinel-Cammell Steam Railbus No.6, which was built for the Southern Railway to the requirements of Mr.R.E.L.Maunsell, for service on the Devils Dyke branch in Sussex, arrived for work on the Westerham branch. This unusual vehicle was not popular, and was soon replaced by push and pull trains, worked by R and R1 class 0-4-4Ts, followed in the 1950's by the ever faithful Wainwright H class 0-4-4T's, which were to work the line until it closed.

Although losing money for many years, the line was still considered a necessary means of transport for the commuters travelling to and from London. Unfortunately, rumours of the forthcoming Southern Orbital Road (now the M25) put the future of the branch in some doubt, and despite protests, Mr.Ernest Marples, the then Minister of Transport, took the decision in August 1961 to close the line. The last day's service was on Saturday October 28th 1961.

Some while before closure, the Westerham Branch Railway Passenger's Association had been formed to try to save the line, and even though they were unsuccessful, they soon put forward plans to reopen the branch after it closed. Unfortunately, with so many obstacles put in the way, this unique opportunity of a Railway Association actually running a railway, never materialised.

H class 0-4-4T No.31193 with push and pull set at Westerham Station. November 12th 1955.

A.E.Bennett

Chevening Halt. September 15th 1957.   A.E.Bennett

O1 class 0-6-0 No.1048 at Brasted Station with the branch train.   The late H.C.Casserley

The Dungeness & New Romney Branch

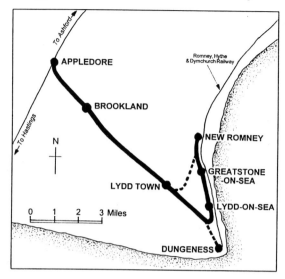

The first real signs of a possible railway to New Romney came in July 1866, when a line from Appledore, on the main SER Ashford to Hastings line, was authorised as the New Romney Railway, but powers were later abandoned.

In the early 1870's, Dungeness was being looked at as a possible port and, in 1873, the Rye and Dungeness Railway & Pier Company was incorporated, to build a line from Rye to Dungeness, where (as the title of the company suggests) they would build a pier. Neither the railway nor the pier were built and in 1875, the powers were passed to the SER.

By the end of the 1870's, Sir Edward Watkin was very keen to build a harbour at Dungeness and had grand ideas of a new cross-channel steamer service between Dungeness and the French fishing port of Le Tréport, 114 miles by rail from Paris. If a new rail route could be developed between London and Dungeness, it was claimed that this route between London and Paris would be shorter than any other.

With all this in mind, the nominally independent Lydd Railway Company was formed, and on April 8th 1881 were authorised to build a standard gauge single track line from Appledore to Lydd, with an intermediate station at Brookland, and then on to a terminus at Dungeness. The line was to be worked by the SER and the chairman of the new Lydd Railway Company was Alfred Mellor Watkin, son of the SER's Sir Edward Watkin. The engineer appointed by the company was SER's Francis Brady while the contractor was T.A.Walker.

The line was opened for passengers from Appledore to Lydd on December 7th 1881 and to Dungeness on the same day, but for goods only.

On July 24th 1882, the company was authorised to build an extension from just south of Lydd Station to New Romney, and also build a northern extension from Appledore to Headcorn via Tenterden. Later, a further line from Headcorn to Loose, near Maidstone, was authorised on January 25th 1883.

The section from Lydd to Dungeness was opened for passengers on April 1st 1883, and the New Romney extension was opened for both passenger and goods service on June 19th 1884. The northern section was never built, and on June 21st

1892, powers were passed to the SER, who in January 1895 absorbed the Lydd Railway Company.

After holiday camp development took place along the coast between Littlestone-on-Sea and Dungeness, the Southern Railway (the new owners of the line) decided to re-site the New Romney branch nearer to the sea, with new stations at Lydd-on-Sea and Greatstone-on-Sea. The new alignment was brought into use on June 4th 1937, when the original line from near Lydd to New Romney was abandoned. Lydd Station was renamed Lydd Town at this time.

The Dungeness section was closed for passengers at the same time, although remained open for goods until May 1953.

As time went on, the grand plans for a port at Dungeness were never to materialise and the northern extension from Appledore to Maidstone was never built, although the Kent & East Sussex Railway did build an extension from their line at Tenterden to Headcorn in 1905, and even planned to extend from Headcorn to Maidstone although, like the Lydd Railway Company, they never did.

In 1964 the goods depot at New Romney was closed and on March 6th 1967, the passenger service on the branch was withdrawn and the line between Lydd Town and New Romney closed completely. Surprisingly, the goods service continued to be handled at Lydd Town until October 4th 1971.

The track is still in position as far as Romney Junction (the site of the re-alignment) and serves the Dungeness Power Station, but from here the original line to Dungeness and the branch to New Romney are just a memory.

Early motive power ranged from Cudworth 2-4-0's to Standard Goods 0-6-0's, followed by Stirling A, B and F class 4-4-0's, and O and O1 class 0-6-0's (the latter two locomotives also working goods trains). The early part of the century saw Kirtley H class 0-6-0's, R class 0-4-4T's and M class 4-4-0's, as well as the Wainwright designed Steam Railcars. During the 1920's Wainwright H class 0-4-4T's saw extensive use on the branch.

In the 1930's the Southern Railway experimented with a petrol engined Railcar on the branch, but later sold it in 1934 to the Weston, Clevedon and Portishead Light Railway. The late 1930's saw Billingham E4 class 0-6-2T's on the branch, while the 1940's and 50's saw Billingham D3 class 0-4-4T's also in service.

Lydd Station soon after the line opened. This station was later renamed Lydd Town after the new alignment to New Romney was brought into use.   Lens of Sutton

Through weekend trains from Charing Cross were mainly handled by Wainwright L class 4-4-0's, although occasionally 'Schools' and 'West Country' classes were used.

The 1950's and 60's saw the return of the ever faithful Wainwright H class 0-4-4T's, who shared duties with B.R. Standard Class 2 Tanks 2-6-2T's, while the goods trains were in the hands of Wainwright C class 0-6-0's.

The passenger service in the last years of operation was provided by 2 and 3 car diesel electric units, although 6 car 'Hastings' type sets worked the through service from Charing Cross.

D.654.2 approaching Lydd-on-Sea with the New Romney-Ashford train. August 7th 1961.

J.J.Smith

H class 0-4-4T No.162 at New Romney Station. October 17th 1929.   The late H.C.Casserley

The Port Victoria & Allhallows Branch

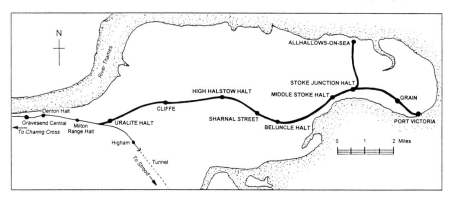

The rather lonely peninsula known as the Hundred of Hoo and the Isle of Grain, which lies to the north of the Medway towns, was not really a great attraction from a railway point of view until 1864, when a scheme was put forward by a group of local people who saw the potential for a pier on the River Medway, directly opposite Sheerness on the Isle of Sheppey, and a railway to serve it. This scheme was known as the North Kent Extension Railway, and would run from a junction at Denton on the main SER North Kent line, east of Gravesend, across the peninsula to the Isle of Grain. Naturally enough, both the SER and the LCDR opposed this scheme, and although powers were obtained in 1865 to build the line, enthusiasm for the railway soon faded and the line was never built.

When in 1876 the LCDR opened a short branch on the Isle of Sheppey from their Sheerness line to Queenborough Pier, and started a new cross-channel service between Queenborough and Flushing in Holland, the SER quickly supported the Hundred of Hoo Railway Company (HoHR), who aimed to build a line from a junction at Shorne Marshes near Higham on the North Kent Railway, across the Hoo peninsula, with stations at Cliffe and Sharnel Street, to the village of Stoke.

This line was authorised on July 21st 1879 and the SER not only agreed to work the single track line, but also backed the HoHR for an extension from Stoke to a point on the coast of the Isle of Grain, directly opposite Queenborough, where a pier would also be built, with the railway terminating there.

The engineer was the SER's Francis Brady and the contractor for the original section from the junction with the North Kent line to Stoke was George Furness, while the contractor for the remaining section from Stoke to the shore of the Isle of Grain, plus the building of the pier was T.A.Walker. The SER absorbed the HoHR in 1881 and had decided to call the terminus Port Victoria.

The line was opened from Hoo Junction to Sharnal Street on April 1st 1882, and from Sharnal Street to Port Victoria on September 11th 1882.

Although Port Victoria was not an instant success, a ferry service was opened to Sheerness, and the new port quickly became popular with the Royal Family and many Royal visitors from overseas, who found that the port was ideally situated, in an isolated spot, and was quite a straight forward route by rail to London. In fact, by 1899 the Royal Corinthian Yacht Club was opened at Port Victoria.

In 1900, the original pier at Queenborough was burned down, and for some months the Flushing steamers from Holland used Port Victoria.

In 1906, several wooden halts were opened between Hoo Junction and Port

Victoria in conjunction with the use of Wainwright's Steam Railcars. These new halts were at Uralite, High Halstow, Beluncle, Middle Stoke and Grain Crossing.

All branch trains ran from Gravesend on the North Kent line via halts at Milton Road, Denton and Milton Range (all opened at the same time as the halts on the branch), before leaving the main line at Hoo Junction.

By 1916, the pier at Port Victoria was considered unsafe and all trains terminated at the beginning of the pier. In 1932 the station on the pier closed completely and was replaced by a new wooden platform at the approach to the pier.

In the 1920's, the Southern Railway decided to create a new seaside resort at Allhallows on the north of the peninsula, and build a new line from their Port Victoria branch to serve it. This new line, which was authorised in June 1929, would run from a junction between Middle Stoke and Grain Crossing Halt, to be known as Stoke Junction. Work started in August 1931 - the resident engineer was R.C.Coward and the contractor was a firm called Robertson.

The line to Allhallows opened on May 14th 1932 as a single track, but was double between Stoke Junction and Allhallows in 1934.

After World War II, the whole site at Port Victoria was taken over by a large oil refinery and a new station was provided at Grain, just east of Grain Crossing Halt, and opened on September 4th 1951, while both Port Victoria and Grain Crossing Halt had closed on June 10th 1951.

The hope of Allhallows developing into a major seaside resort (it was named Allhallows-on-Sea, even though it was actually on the Thames) never materialised and the line between Stoke Junction and Allhallows was singled in 1957.

In the early 1960's, British Railways decided to withdraw all passenger trains on the branch which meant that the Allhallows section would close completely. The final day for the passenger service was December 2nd 1961, although, unlike all the other lines mentioned in this publication (with the exception of a section of the Dungeness branch) this line is still open at the time of writing, carrying oil, ballast, cement and many other items from this rather strange area of Kent.

When the line first opened, there is no doubt that Cudworth 2-4-0 locomotives were used, and were soon followed by Stirling Q and Q1 class 0-4-4T's and O and O1 class 0-6-0's. Later came Kirtley R and R1 class 0-4-4T's, Wainwright H class 0-4-4T's and C class 0-6-0's, as well as the previously mentioned Steam Railcars. In later years the passenger service saw Bulleid Q1 class 0-6-0's, which also worked oil trains from the Isle of Grain. The final years of the passenger service, like most similar branch lines in Kent, saw the return of Wainwright H class 0-4-4T's.

Allhallows-on-Sea Station. August 23rd 1955.

R.M.Casserley

A train approaching Grain from Port Victoria.

An unidentified Q class 0-4-4T waits on the pier station at Port Victoria while the railway staff pose for the photograph.

The Gravesend West Branch

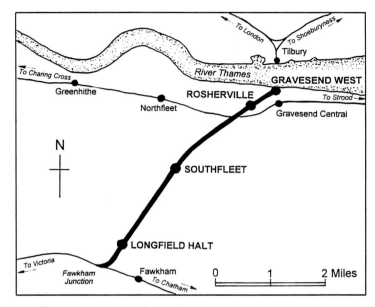

In 1845, the Thames & Medway Canal Company laid a single track railway along the canal's tow path between Gravesend and Strood. Some four years later, the SER purchased the Canal Company and converted the canal into a double track railway which helped to form part of their North Kent line.

About five miles south of Gravesend, the LCDR opened their main line from London to the Medway towns.

In 1881, a branch line from the LCDR main line, between Farningham Road and Fawkham stations to Gravesend, with intermediate stations at Southfleet and Rosherville, was proposed, known as the Gravesend Railway. Although promoted as an independent company, it was fully supported by the LCDR, who would work the line. On July 18th 1881, the Gravesend Railway Company was authorised to build a double track railway from the LCDR main line, at a point which became known as Fawkham Junction, to Gravesend via Southfleet and Rosherville. At about the same time, the London, Tilbury & Southend Railway had planned to build a tunnel under the Thames so that their line from Tilbury could link up with the Gravesend Railway, and also the SER at Gravesend. Although the tunnel and railway were never built, the Gravesend Railway was authorised on July 24th 1882, to construct a pier on the Thames and extend the plans for their new line to run from it..

The engineer appointed by the Gravesend Railway was C.D.Fox and the contractor was G.Barclay-Bruce. On June 29th 1883, the Gravesend Railway was taken over by the LCDR and their chief engineer William Mills appears to have taken over from C.D.Fox.

The line officially opened on April 17th 1886 (the same day that Tilbury Docks opened), although it was not until May 10th 1886 that it actually opened to the public.

One hopeful source of revenue for the new line was the pleasure gardens at Rosherville and, with the possibility of boat trains to serve the pier at Gravesend, the future of the line looked very promising.

When the SER and the LCDR developed their working relationship in 1899, the LCDR station at Gravesend became known as Gravesend West Street to avoid confusion with the SER station at Gravesend which later became known as Gravesend Central.

From when the line opened, all trains ran through from London, including an express service to link with various steamers which called at the pier from London on their way to Southend, Clacton, Walton on the Naze, and then back to London via Gravesend.

Although the line had several industrial sidings, the final closure of the Rosherville Pleasure Gardens in 1910 was a big blow to the passenger future of the line. In 1913, when push-and-pull trains were introduced as an economic measure, a halt at Longfield (which was situated between Fawkham Junction and Southfleet) was opened.

In 1916, the Dutch Batavia line opened a regular boat service between the pier at Gravesend and Rotterdam. This new service meant that a boat train was introduced from Victoria to the pier. By 1939, through trains from London, with the exception of the boat trains, had ceased and the service became, purely local by running to and from Swanley or Farningham Road.

After the Second World War, the Batavia line steamers, which were suspended while the hostilities were taking place, resumed although to Tilbury and not Gravesend. Pleasure trips run by the General Steam Navigation, were taking place in the 1950's and at about the same time, the word "Street" was dropped from the title of the branch, which from then on, became known as Gravesend West branch line.

Passenger trains were withdrawn from the branch on Monday August 3rd 1953 and in 1959 the line was singled. On March 24th 1968 the goods service was also withdrawn and the line closed.

It is unclear which locomotives worked the passenger service when the line opened, but Kirtley R class 0-4-4T's were in use during the later part of the 1890's. In 1913, Wainwright H class 0-4-4Ts were working push-and pull local trains between Swanley and Gravesend West Street, followed by Wainwright P class 0-6-0T's. In 1916, R class 0-4-4T's were back on the line working the local service, and were soon joined by the R1 class 0-4-4T's. During the 1930's, the former London & South Western Railway Drummond M7 class 0-4-4T's were also put to use on the line.

C class 0-6-0 No. 1576 with the Rotterdam boat train at Gravesend West Station. July 23rd 1938.
The late H.C.Casserley

Southfleet Station, looking north. November 21st 1959.   J.J.Smith

Rosherville Station, looking north to Gravesend West. November 21st 1959.   J.J.Smith

Looking across the River Thames to Tilbury from Gravesend West Station. November 21st 1959.

J.J.Smith

The Elham Valley Railway

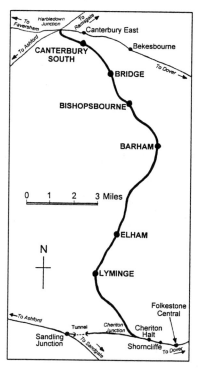

The Elham Valley Railway Company was incorporated in 1864 to build a line from Canterbury to Folkestone but, nothing happened until the LCDR sought permission in 1883 to reach Folkestone by building a branch from their station at Kearsney on the main Canterbury to Dover line.

Although this proposal was rejected, to make sure that the LCDR never tried again, the SER took over the Elham Valley Railway Company in 1884 so that they could build this line as a security.

The line was to be double track and nearly 17 miles long, and would run from a junction on the main Ashford to Folkestone line at Cheriton, to a junction at Harbledown, on the main Ashford to Ramsgate line, with intermediate stations at Lyminge, Elham, Barham, Bishopsbourne, Bridge and Canterbury South. The engineer was the SER's Francis Brady and the appointed contractor was T.A.Walker.

The line was opened from Cheriton Junction to Barham on July 4th 1887 and was completely opened through to Harbledown Junction on July 1st 1889.

From when it was first opened, the line continued in a general uneventful way until the 1914-18 war when, due to a landslip near the Martello Tunnel on the main line near Folkestone, the Elham Valley line became the only means of rail transport between Folkestone and Dover.

In 1916, the line was temporarily singled, but was reinstated as a double track railway soon after the war was over. From this time onwards, the line returned to normal pre-war atmosphere, although a regular bus service was introduced in 1919, which ran through the valley on a parallel road to the railway and, in October 1931, the section of line from Harbledown Junction to Lyminge was singled.

During World War II, the line was completely taken over by the War Department who kept a vast rail-mounted gun in Bishopsbourne Tunnel.

On Friday December 1st 1940, the passenger service north of Lyminge was withdrawn, and although a normal service remained between Folkestone and Lyminge, the War Department took over the running of the daily goods service.

On February 16th 1945, the goods service returned to the control of the Southern Railway, and although the passenger service continued to Lyminge, the locals still hoped that they would soon have their through service to Canterbury restored.

Unfortunately, like so many similar lines at this time, with competition from road transport, the Elham Valley had really "had its day" and the Southern Railway decided, despite protests from the Elham Valley District Council, to close the line completely on and from June 16th 1947.

Early motive power was handled by Cudworth's 118 class 2-4-0's and Stirling O class 0-6-0's, followed by Stirling Q class 0-4-4T's, Wainwright H class 0-4-4T's and C class 0-6-0's, and later Maunsall N class 2-6-0's and Wainwright J class 0-6-4T's. Wainwright Steam Railcars were also briefly used from Folkestone to Elham.

Barham Station

Lens of Sutton

An early view of shunting taking place in the siding at Lyminge Station.

Author's Collection

Bishopsbourne Station in 1936.

H class 0-4-4T No.1161 at Lyminge. May 24th 1947.

The Chatham Central Branch

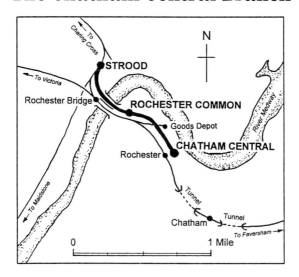

With railways fast developing in Kent, the Medway towns quickly became an attraction, and in February 1845, the Gravesend & Rochester Railway & Canal Company began running trains through the Higham canal tunnel to Strood, from were steam boats connected the Strood Station with the Blue Boar and Sun Piers at Rochester and Chatham. This company was acquired by the SER in 1846 and later extended the line from Strood to Maidstone, although both Rochester and Chatham still had to make do with steam boats and horse bus connections.

In 1858, the SER's great rivals, the East Kent Railway, who became the LCDR in 1859, extended their line from London over the River Medway to Chatham, and this new route quickly took away traffic from the SER's Strood Station.

In 1873 the SER contemplated their own route from Strood over the River Medway to Chatham but, because of the finance involved, nothing happened, although a connecting spur between the LCDR and the SER was built at the south end of Strood Station. This spur was only used for goods traffic until Mr. Toomer, the Mayor of Rochester, complained to the Railway Commission and, from April 1877 the SER ran a through passenger service to the LCDR's Chatham Station.

The SER chairman Sir Edward Watkin was not entirely happy with this situation and in 1881 he revised the 1873 suggestion for the SER to have their own line from Strood to Chatham. The line was authorised on August 11th 1881 and the SER had to also obtain the permission of the Admiralty and the Medway Conservators to build across the river. Although these powers lapsed, they were revived again in 1887 and the whole branch was built by the SER's workforce, with the exception of the river bridge and the brick ports of the viaduct, which was built by John Cochrane & Sons.

The line was opened from Strood to Rochester Common, the only intermediate station on July 20th 1891, and through to the terminus at Chatham Central on March 1st 1892. Most of the branch was on a viaduct while the river bridge was on four piers, parallel with not only the LCDR's bridge, but also a road bridge.

The branch was double track, only just over 1 mile long, and surprisingly enough, Chatham Central Station was actually in Rochester.

29

Early locomotive power on the branch is unclear but it is known that in 1909, Wainwright P class 0-6-0T's were in use on the line and were followed by his Steam Railcars. Kirtley R class 0-4-4T's also saw service at about this time.

After the formation of the South Eastern & Chatham Railway Management Committee, the Chatham Central branch was doomed and the line closed completely on and from October 1st 1911. The wooden viaducts were demolished in 1913, as was Rochester Common Station. The SER line now joined the LCDR line to the east of the river and all trains used the SER bridge, although in 1919, after it was damaged by fire, the SER bridge was temporarily closed and the original loop, which became known as the Toomer loop (after the former mayor of Rochester), was brought back into existence.

In 1927, the Southern Railway made arrangements that all trains would use the SER bridge, although in 1942, the LCDR bridge was strengthened so that it could be used in an emergency, should the SER bridge be damaged by bombs. Later the LCDR bridge was demolished to make way for a new road bridge which opened in 1970.

Rochester Common Station during demolition. E.Course Collection

Steam Railcar No.2 at Chatham Central Station. Lens of Sutton

Conclusion

The branch lines in Kent have now passed into history and like so many similar branch lines and light railways throughout the country are just a memory from long ago. The local community took their railway for granted and thought it was with them for ever but, time moves on and modern transport in the form of buses and cars have now taken the place of the lovable branch line train which would set out in all weather across lonely fields and through cuttings to link villages with towns and pick up the passengers who relied on the railway as their only means of travel.

Several branch lines have been preserved by enthusiasts to try and re-create those timeless days for a younger generation. In Kent (as mentioned in my companion publication *"The Col. Stephens Railways in Kent"*) the Kent & East Sussex Railway is now in the hands of the Tenterden Railway Company who have set about restoring part of the line to some of its former glory.

The long standing feud between the SER and the LCDR is now very much a time from the past but it is interesting to look back and wonder what the situation might be today if the channel tunnel had been built when Sir Edward Watkin had planned it. He would certainly find it hard to understand why it took so long.

H class 0-4-4T No.1305 is seen here leaving the remote station at Brookland with the branch train for New Romney.

The late H.C.Casserley

Acknowledgments

I would like to thank the following people for their kind help in supplying photographs for this publication: Mr.J.J.Smith, Mr.A.E.Bennett, Mr.R.M.Casserley, Mr.R.F.Roberts, Mr.J.H.Meredith, Dr.E.Course and last but not least Mr.J.L.Smith of Lens of Sutton.

My thanks to my son Paul for reading my text and also to James Christian of Binfield Printers Ltd.

Bibliography

FORGOTTEN RAILWAYS: SOUTH-EAST ENGLAND by H.P.White (David & Charles)
THE RAILWAYS OF SOUTHERN ENGLAND: SECONDARY AND BRANCH LINES
by Edwin Course (Batsford)
THE LONDON, CHATHAM & DOVER RAILWAY by Adrain Gray (Meresborough Books)
SOUTH EASTERN RAILWAY by Adrain Gray (Middleton Press)
BRANCH LINES OF THE SOUTHERN RAILWAY Vol. 2
by George Reeve & Chris Hawkins (Wild Swan)
BYGONE SOUTH EASTERN STEAM Vol. 4 - CLOSED BRANCH LINES
by A.R.L. Ratcliffe (Rochester Press)
THE CANTERBURY & WHITSTABLE RAILWAY by Brian Hart (Wild Swan)
THE CANTERBURY & WHITSTABLE RAILWAY by Ivan Maxted (Oakwood Press)
THE HYTHE & SANDGATE RAILWAY by Brian Hart (Wild Swan)
THE WESTERHAM VALLEY RAILWAY by David Gould (Oakwood Press)
THE HUNDRED OF HOO RAILWAY by Brian Hart (Wild Swan)
ISLE OF GRAIN RAILWAYS by Adrian Gray (Oakwood Press)
THE GRAVESEND WEST BRANCH by N.Pallant (Oakwood Press)
SOUTHERN RAILWAY BRANCH LINES IN THE THIRTIES
by R.W.Kidner (Oakwood Press)
SOUTHERN RAILWAY BRANCH LINE TRAINS by R.W.Kidner (Oakwood Press)

Q1 class 0-6-0 No.33029 dubbed the "Westerham Flyer", approaching Chevening Halt with a special six coach corridor train for the final day of operation on the Westerham branch. October 28th 1961.   A.E.Bennett